Jack C. Richard dy

Passages
Third Edition

Workbook 1 A

CAMBRIDGE
UNIVERSITY PRESS

CAMBRIDGE
UNIVERSITY PRESS

University Printing House, Cambridge CB2 8BS, United Kingdom

One Liberty Plaza, 20th Floor, New York, NY 10006, USA

477 Williamstown Road, Port Melbourne, VIC 3207, Australia

314–321, 3rd Floor, Plot 3, Splendor Forum, Jasola District Centre, New Delhi – 110025, India

79 Anson Road, #06–04/06, Singapore 079906

Cambridge University Press is part of the University of Cambridge.

It furthers the University's mission by disseminating knowledge in the pursuit of education, learning and research at the highest international levels of excellence.

www.cambridge.org
Information on this title: www.cambridge.org/9781107627185

First published 1998
Second edition 2008
Reprinted 2019

Printed in Italy by Rotolito S.p.A.

A catalog record for this publication is available from the British Library

ISBN 978-1-107-62705-5 Student's Book 1
ISBN 978-1-107-62701-7 Student's Book 1A
ISBN 978-1-107-62706-2 Student's Book 1B
ISBN 978-1-107-62725-3 Workbook 1
ISBN 978-1-107-62718-5 Workbook 1A
ISBN 978-1-107-62720-8 Workbook 1B
ISBN 978-1-107-62768-0 Teacher's Edition 1 with Assessment Audio CD/CD-ROM
ISBN 978-1-107-62754-3 Class Audio 1 CDs
ISBN 978-1-107-62769-7 Full Contact 1
ISBN 978-1-107-62771-0 Full Contact 1A
ISBN 978-1-107-62772-7 Full Contact 1B
ISBN 978-1-107-62762-8 DVD 1
ISBN 978-1-107-66626-9 Presentation Plus 1

Additional resources for this publication at www.cambridge.org/passages

Book design: Q2A / Bill Smith
Art direction, layout services and photo research: Tighe Publishing Services

Contents

Credits iv

1 Friends and family 1

2 Mistakes and mysteries 7

3 Exploring new cities 13

4 Early birds and night owls 19

5 Communication 25

6 What's the real story? 31

Credits

Illustration credits

Kim Johnson: 4, 28, 45, 66, 67
Dan McGeehan: 7, 54
Paul Hostetler: 8, 27, 56, 60, 64
Koren Shadmi: 33, 52, 62
James Yamasaki: 22, 35, 61

Photography credits

1 ©Chris Bennett/Aurora/Getty Images; **3** (*clockwise from top center*) ©Keith Levit/Design Pics/Corbis, ©iStock/Thinkstock, ©Iconica/Commercial Eye/Getty Images; **6** ©Barry Austin Photography/Getty Images; **9** ©iStock/Thinkstock; **10** ©dieKleinert/Alamy; **11** ©Holger Hollemann/dpa/picture-alliance/Newscom; **12** ©Christian Guy/Getty Images; **13** ©iStock/Thinkstock; **14** ©iStock/Thinkstock; **15** ©iStock/Thinkstock; **16** ©John W Banagan/Photographer's Choice/Getty Images; **18** (*top left to right*) ©trekandshoot/Shutterstock, ©iStock/Thinkstock, ©iStock.com/wdstock, ©A. T. Willett/Alamy; (*bottom*) ©Rudolf Balasko/Thinkstock; **20** ©Media Bakery; **23** ©Blue Jean Images/Alamy; **24** ©andresrimaging/iStockphoto; **26** ©Pulp Photography/The Image Bank/Getty Images; **29** ©iStock/Thinkstock; **30** ©Clover/SuperStock; **31** ©Eric Isselee/Shutterstock; **34** ©Elke Meitzel/age fotostock; **36** (*top to bottom*) ©assalave/iStockphoto, ©Antonio Balaguer soler/Thinkstock; **38** ©iStock/Thinkstock; **40** ©Wavebreak Media/Thinkstock; **41** ©iStock.com/DSGpro; **44** (*left to right*) ©Jodi/Jake/Media Bakery, ©Masterfile Royalty Free, ©Andresr/age fotostock; **46** ©Caspar Benson/fstop/Corbis; **47** (*left to right*) ©wavebreakmedia/Shutterstock, ©Juanmonino/E+/Getty Images, ©iStock.com/pressureUA, ©homydesign/Shutterstock; **48** (*top*) Janos Levente/Shutterstock, (*center*) Sofi photo/Shutterstock; **49** ©Masterfile Royalty Free; **50** (*clockwise from top left*) Suprijono Suharjoto/Thinkstock, Blend Images/SuperStock, Jack Hollingsworth/Thinkstock, Jupiterimages/Thinkstock; **53** ©Mitchell Funk/Photographer's Choice/Getty Images; **56** ©Stockbyte/Thinkstock; **59** (*left to right*) ©Enrique Algarra/age fotostock, ©Dan Brownsword/Cultura/Getty Images, ©Masterfile Royalty Free; **63** ©Vicki Reid/E+/Getty Images; **68** ©Iakov Kalinin/Shutterstock; **70** Arvind Balaraman/Thinkstock; **71** (*left to right*) ©Greg Epperson/Shutterstock, ©Image Source/age fotostock; **Back cover:** (*clockwise from top*) ©Leszek Bogdewicz/Shutterstock, ©Wavebreak Media/Thinkstock, ©Blend Images/Alamy, ©limpido/Shutterstock

Text credits

The authors and publishers acknowledge the following sources of copyright material and are grateful for the permissions granted. While every effort has been made, it has not always been possible to identify the sources of all the material used, or to trace all copyright holders. If any omissions are brought to our notice, we will be happy to include the appropriate acknowledgments on reprinting.

48 Adapted from "Everyday Creativity," by Carlin Flora, *Psychology Today,* November 1, 2009. Psychology Today © Copyright 2005, www.Psychologytoday.com; **54** Adapted from "Why We Dream: Real Reasons Revealed," by Rachael Rettner, *LiveScience,* June 27, 2010. Reproduced with permission of LiveScience; **60** Adapted from "The Survival Guide for Dealing with Chronic Complainers," by Guy Winch, PhD, *Psychology Today*, July 15, 2011. Reproduced with permission of Guy Winch, www.guywinch.com; **66** Adapted from "Internet On, Inhibitions Off: Why We Tell All," by Matt Ridley, *The Wall Street Journal,* February 18, 2012. Reproduced with permission of The Wall Street Journal. Copyright © 2012 Dow Jones & Company, Inc. All Rights Reserved Worldwide; **72** Adapted from "International Careers: A World of Opportunity: Battling Culture Shock Starts with Trip to Local Bookstores, Seminars: Advance preparation is critical in adjusting to the challenges of life in a foreign country," by Karen E. Klein, *Los Angeles Times*, September 11, 1995. Copyright © 1995. Los Angeles Times. Reprinted with permission.

1 FRIENDS AND FAMILY

LESSON A ▶ *What kind of person are you?*

1 GRAMMAR

Which verbs and expressions can complete the sentences?
Write the correct numbers of the sentences next to the verbs.

1. I _____ spending time outdoors.

2. I _____ to spend time outdoors.

a. __1__ am afraid of   g. ____ feel like

b. ____ am into   h. ____ hate

c. ____ avoid   i. ____ insist on

d. ____ can't stand   j. _1, 2_ love

e. ____ don't mind   k. ____ prefer

f. ____ enjoy   l. ____ worry about

2 GRAMMAR

Read the conversations and complete the sentences using the gerund or infinitive form of
the verb. If the two forms are possible, write both of them.

1. Ada: Sam isn't happy when he has nothing to do.

   Gary: I know. It really bothers him.

   Sam can't stand *having nothing to do / to have nothing to do.* _____

2. Vic: I hardly ever go to school parties anymore.

   Joon: Me neither. They're not as much fun as they used to be.

   Vic and Joon avoid _____

3. Tina: You visit your parents on the weekends, don't you?

   Leo: Yes, I visit them on Sundays so I can spend the whole day with them.

   Leo prefers _____

4. Tom: Are you going to take an Italian class this summer?

   Ivy: Yes, I am. I love to learn new languages.

   Ivy is into _____

5. Ang: Do you want to go rock climbing with me this weekend?

   Sue: I don't know. Rock climbing sounds dangerous!

   Sue is worried about _____

6. Josh: What sort of volunteer work do you do for the library, Celia?

   Celia: I love to read to kids, so I volunteer as a storyteller on Saturdays.

   Celia enjoys _____

3 GRAMMAR

Write sentences about yourself using the verbs and expressions in the box.
Use the gerund of the verbs in the phrases below.

| am afraid of | avoid | don't mind | hate | love |
| am into | can't stand | enjoy | insist on | prefer |

1. go shopping on the weekend

   I love going shopping on the weekend.

2. try different types of food

   _____

3. learn new sports or hobbies

   _____

4. meet new people

   _____

5. work on the weekend

   _____

6. clean and organize my room

   _____

4 VOCABULARY

A Match the words to make logical sentences.

1. Angelina volunteers at a hospital. She's very _b_ .   a. wild and crazy
2. Stan drives too fast and stays out late. He's _____.   b. kind and generous
3. Anna never gets angry. She's always _____.   c. shy and reserved
4. Don hates a messy room. He likes being _____.   d. friendly and outgoing
5. Tad avoids speaking out in class. He's _____.   e. calm and cool
6. Neil loves throwing parties and making his guests   f. neat and tidy
   feel welcome. He's _____.
                                                           g. honest and sincere
7. City life is crazy! In the country, I feel more _____. h. laid-back and relaxed
8. Julia insists on doing things her way. She's _____.   i. strong and independent
9. Mei never hides her true feelings. She's always _____.

B Use the vocabulary above to write sentences about people you know.

1. *My sister is shy and reserved. She avoids meeting new people.*
2. _____
3. _____
4. _____
5. _____
6. _____

5 WRITING

A Choose the main idea for each paragraph, and write it in the blank below.

> My mother loves speaking Chinese.
>
> My mother is very adventurous.
>
> I really admire my mother.
>
> I am not like my mother at all.

1. _____. She enjoys doing unusual things and pushing herself to the limit. Last year, for example, she insisted on visiting China. She enrolled in Chinese language classes, planned her trip, and then took off across China with a friend. She loves exploring new places, and she doesn't hesitate to start conversations with locals wherever she goes.

> I have a friend named John.
>
> My friend John and I are in the same class.
>
> My friend John is the kind of person who loves to talk.
>
> My friend John always says what is on his mind.

2. _____. He's probably the most outspoken person I know. Last week after class, for example, he said to our English teacher, "Some of the students are a little confused by this week's class, but I have some ideas to help explain it to them. Do you want to hear my suggestions?" John was saying what he thought, and luckily our teacher was willing to listen to him.

B Complete these two sentences. Then choose one of them, and write a paragraph to support it.

1. My friend _____ is the kind of person who _____

_____

2. _____ is the most _____ person I know.

_____
_____
_____
_____
_____
_____

GRAMMAR

Read the blog entry. Then underline the noun clauses.

May 15, 2014

I love my family so much, and I really get along with everyone – my parents and my four brothers and sisters. However, sometimes they drive me crazy. There are both good and bad things about coming from a large family. One of the best things about coming from a large family is <u>that I always have someone to talk to</u>. Unfortunately, one of the disadvantages is that I never have any privacy. And of course, the trouble with not having any privacy is that I never have any space I can call my own. Our house is big, but sometimes not big enough!

GRAMMAR

Combine each pair of sentences into one sentence using noun clauses.

1. I'm the youngest in my family. The best thing is I'm the center of attention.
   The best thing about being the youngest is that I'm the center of attention.

2. I have a lot of kids. The disadvantage is I can't give each of them the individual attention they want.
   _____
   _____

3. I live with my father-in-law. The problem is we disagree about everything.
   _____
   _____

4. I have two younger sisters. The worst thing is they always want to know all about my personal life.
   _____
   _____

5. I have an identical twin. The trouble is no one can ever tell us apart.
   _____
   _____

3 GRAMMAR

Use noun clauses and your own ideas to complete these sentences.

1. A disadvantage of having siblings who are successful is _that my parents expect me_
   to be successful, too.

2. The problem with having a large family is _____

   _____

3. The best thing about having grandparents is _____

   _____

4. The trouble with being part of a two-income family is _____

   _____

5. One benefit of living far away from your family is _____

   _____

6. The worst thing about taking a family vacation is _____

   _____

7. An advantage of living with siblings is _____

   _____

4 VOCABULARY

Are the statements true or false? Choose the correct answer.

	True	False
Sylvia's mother has a great-uncle named Martin.		
1. Sylvia is Martin's great-granddaughter.	☐	☑
2. Sylvia's mother is Martin's grandniece.	☐	☐
Hal's wife, Nikki, has a sister named Joanne.		
3. Joanne is Hal's sister-in-law.	☐	☐
4. Joanne is Hal's grandmother.	☐	☐
Hugo's niece Diana has a son-in-law named Jason.		
5. Jason's wife is Hugo's granddaughter.	☐	☐
6. Diana is Jason's mother-in-law.	☐	☐
Molly's nephew Tom has a daughter named Jennifer.		
7. Molly is Tom's aunt.	☐	☐
8. Molly is Jennifer's great-aunt.	☐	☐
Irene's father, Roberto, has a grandfather named Eduardo.		
9. Eduardo is Roberto's grandson.	☐	☐
10. Eduardo is Irene's great-grandfather.	☐	☐

5 READING

A Read the article. Then choose the main idea of each paragraph.

Is it Better or Worse to Be an Only Child?

If you are an only child – someone with no brothers or sisters – you have probably been the object of both sympathy and suspicion. "Oh, you poor thing!" some people say. "You must have been so lonely!" Other people might not say much, but you know they are thinking that you are selfish, spoiled, and have no idea how to get along with others. People assume that only children are somehow at a disadvantage because of their lack of siblings, and this idea has probably been around as long as only children have.

Recent studies, however, have shown that the stereotype of the only child is really just a myth. Only children show very little difference from children with siblings, and as adults they are just as likely to be well adjusted. One slight difference they show from children with multiple siblings is that they often score higher on intelligence and achievement tests. But first-born children and those with only one sibling have similar results, so we can't really say this is a characteristic of the only child, either. The one undeniable difference is that only children get more of their parents' time and attention for the simple reason that there are fewer demands on the parents. The same goes for educational opportunities – there tend to be more resources available in single-child households. However, there is little evidence that this has long-term benefits for only children.

For some reason, though, popular opinion and culture seem to have a hard time accepting the fact that only children are just like everyone else. Movies and TV shows still portray "onlies" as socially awkward and expecting to get whatever they ask for. What keeps the stereotype alive? Could it be that most of us have wished – at one point or another – to be an only child? At least we wouldn't have had to deal with siblings playing with our toys, borrowing our clothes, and eating that last piece of cake we had saved for later.

1. First paragraph:
   ☐ a. Only children all wish they had siblings.
   ☐ b. Only children think other children are selfish.
   ☐ c. Many people make assumptions about only children.

2. Second paragraph:
   ☐ a. Only children really are different from children with siblings.
   ☐ b. Only children are basically the same as those with siblings.
   ☐ c. No one has really studied only children.

3. Third paragraph:
   ☐ a. The popular view of only children seems difficult to change.
   ☐ b. The popular view of only children has changed recently.
   ☐ c. The popular view of only children is based on facts.

B Are the statements true or false? Choose the correct answer. Then rewrite the false statements to make them true.

	True	False
1. Some people feel sorry for only children.	☐	☐
2. When only children grow up, they are less sociable than children with siblings.	☐	☐
3. Only children are more intelligent than children with siblings.	☐	☐
4. According to the author, people's ideas about only children need to change.	☐	☐

2 MISTAKES AND MYSTERIES

LESSON A ▶ *Life lessons*

 VOCABULARY

Correct the underlined mistakes in each sentence. Write the correct form of a verb from the box after each sentence. Sometimes more than one answer is possible.

| aggravate | avoid | cause | deal with | identify | ignore | run into | solve |

1. Jim said I <u>solved</u> the problem with my tablet when I spilled water on it.
   caused

2. Grace didn't pay her credit card bill last month. When she didn't pay it again this month, she only <u>ran into</u> her debt problem. _____

3. I always ask Kate for help with math. She can <u>ignore</u> any problem. _____

4. Tim's report was late. He <u>aggravated</u> problems with his computer that he didn't expect. _____

5. John <u>caused</u> his weight problem for years. Now he can't fit into any of his clothes! _____

6. Mike has many problems with his projects at work, so he often stays late to <u>identify</u> them. _____

7. My brother is an amazing auto mechanic. He can look at a car's engine and <u>ignore</u> what is causing problems. _____

8. Pedro <u>identifies</u> problems with computer viruses by updating his antivirus software every week. _____

GRAMMAR

Choose the past modal or phrasal modal of obligation that best completes each sentence.

1. I *wasn't supposed to* / (had to) give Mr. Lee my phone when he caught me texting in class.

2. Eve was worried that she *needed to* / *didn't have to* pass her exam to graduate.

3. Frank *didn't have to* / *was supposed to* take his grandmother to the store, but he wanted to.

4. I *needed to buy* / *shouldn't have bought* these boots, but they were on sale!

5. Bob *was supposed to* / *didn't need to* bring dessert to the party, but he brought an appetizer instead.

6. I *didn't need to* / *was supposed to* clean my apartment before my friend arrived, but I didn't have time.

GRAMMAR

Complete the email with the past modals and phrasal modals of obligation in the box.
Use each modal only once.

| didn't have to | had to | needed to | should have | shouldn't have | was supposed to |

New Message

Hey Ally,

I (1) __was supposed to__ pick up my brother at practice yesterday,
but I forgot. Well, I didn't forget . . . I went to the café instead.
I (2) _____ go, but I wanted to see you guys.
I (3) _____ thought about my brother, but I didn't. When
my mom discovered that my brother (4) _____ walk
home alone, she got upset with me. She said I (5) _____
forgotten about my brother. So now she doesn't trust me. She said I
(6) _____ think about my responsibilities and behave
more responsibly to regain her trust. Anyway, this means I won't be
able to go on the trip with you guys this weekend. I'm so frustrated!
Gigi

GRAMMAR

Use past modals and phrasal modals of obligation to write a sentence for each situation.

1. make a left turn instead of a right turn
   I should have made a left turn
   instead of a right turn.

2. hand in a research paper today
   _____
   _____

3. pick up a friend from the airport
   _____
   _____

4. not eat a big lunch
   _____
   _____

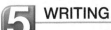

5 WRITING

A Look at the brainstorming notes and add two more ideas to each category.

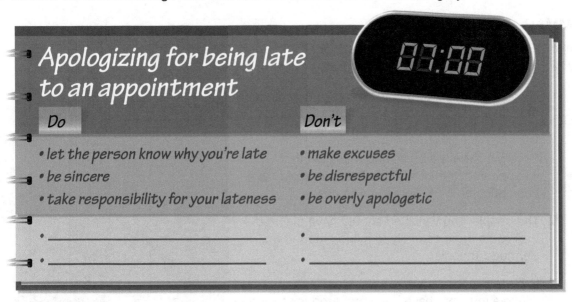

Apologizing for being late to an appointment

Do
- let the person know why you're late
- be sincere
- take responsibility for your lateness
- _____
- _____

Don't
- make excuses
- be disrespectful
- be overly apologetic
- _____
- _____

B Complete the sentences with ideas from your brainstorming notes.

1. You need to _____ when you apologize.
2. You shouldn't _____ when you apologize.

C Choose one of the sentences you completed above and brainstorm supporting ideas for its topic. Then write a paragraph based on your brainstorming notes.

> You shouldn't make excuses when you apologize. You have to simply say you are sorry. For example, if you are late for an appointment, you should never say you were confused about the meeting time. Next, you shouldn't say your directions were bad. In addition, you shouldn't blame public transportation for your lateness. . . .

_____

_____

_____

_____

_____

_____

_____

_____

_____

_____

_____

GRAMMAR

Underline the modals in the sentences. Then write *C* for modals expressing degrees of certainty or *O* for modals expressing obligation, advice, or opinion.

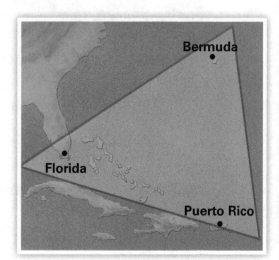

___C___ 1. Some people are certain the boats and airplanes that have disappeared in the Bermuda Triangle <u>must have</u> vanished due to human error.

_____ 2. Others believe the boats and airplanes that disappeared in the Bermuda Triangle could have been affected by supernatural forces.

_____ 3. The people who vanished should have planned their route more carefully to avoid entering the Bermuda Triangle.

_____ 4. Experts say the people who got lost in the Bermuda Triangle must not have been prepared for strong water currents and changing weather patterns.

_____ 5. While many people have successfully navigated through the Bermuda Triangle, there are others who shouldn't have tried, as they are now missing.

GRAMMAR

Choose the phrase that best completes each sentence.

THE **BLOG** SPACE

August 31

I just watched a documentary about the princess who died in a mysterious car accident. It was so interesting – everyone (1) *should watch* / *should have been watching* it. The princess was too young and smart to die in such an awful accident. Many people feel that she (2) *shouldn't have gone* / *may not have been going* in the car that night. Anyway, the documentary said there are many theories about how the car accident happened. Some people think the car's brakes (3) *might have been tampered* / *should have tampered* with. Others believe that the princess's driver (4) *should have caused* / *could have caused* the accident. Some even think the princess (5) *could have been kidnapped* / *could have kidnapped*. The police never figured out what really happened. I'm not sure what to believe, but there (6) *shouldn't have been* / *must have been* a way to solve this mystery!

Comments (4)

GRAMMAR

Use modals expressing degrees of certainty and your own ideas to write about the following situations.

1. Your friend got the highest grade on a difficult English exam.

   He must have studied really hard. It's also possible the test may have been too easy.

   _____

2. You don't hear from your best friend for several days.

   _____

   _____

3. Your favorite jacket isn't in your closet.

   _____

   _____

4. You see some very large footprints while walking in the park.

   _____

   _____

4 VOCABULARY

Use the verbs of belief in the box to write a sentence about each topic.

assume	be sure	figure	know for a fact
be certain	bet	guess	suppose
be positive	doubt	have a hunch	suspect

1. Elephants are the world's smartest animals.

   I am sure that elephants are the world's

   smartest animals.

2. There is a monster that lives in Loch Ness in Scotland.

   _____

   _____

3. Global warming is causing changes in worldwide weather patterns.

   _____

4. People eat bananas more than any other fruit in the world.

   _____

5. Some pyramids were built more than 2,000 years ago.

   _____

6. Dinosaurs were wiped out by an asteroid that caused changes in the climate.

   _____

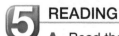

A Read the article quickly to find the answers to the questions.

1. When did the British couple go on vacation? _____

2. Who gave the couple directions to Spain? _____

Hotel Time Warp

The idea of traveling backward or forward through time has long been a favorite subject of books, movies, and TV shows. Although some scientists suspect that it may actually be possible, no one has invented a way to make it happen. However, many people have reported traveling in time.

One famous story is about a British couple who were vacationing in France in 1979. They were looking for a place to stay for the night and noticed a sign for an old circus. They found a hotel nearby and discovered that almost everything inside the hotel was made of heavy wood and there were no modern conveniences such as telephones or TVs. Furthermore, their room doors did not have locks, and the windows had wooden shutters instead of glass. In the morning, two police officers entered the hotel wearing old-fashioned uniforms with capes. After getting confusing directions from the officers to Spain, the couple paid their amazingly inexpensive hotel bill and left.

Two weeks later, the couple returned to France and decided to stay at the odd, but very cheap, hotel again. This time, however, the hotel was nowhere to be found. Positive that they were in the exact same spot because of the circus posters, the couple realized that the hotel had completely vanished. Even more confusing, they found that the photographs they had taken inside the hotel did not develop. Later, their research uncovered that the French officers had been wearing uniforms dating from before 1905.

Researchers analyzing these events call them "time slips" and believe that they must happen randomly and spontaneously. However, researchers cannot explain why, when, or how they occur. But when they do occur, people are so bewildered and confused that they can barely explain what happened to them, even though they are sure they have experienced some sort of time travel.

B Read the article again. Choose the statements you think the author would agree with.

☐ 1. Time travel is not a favorite subject of books, movies, and television shows.

☐ 2. Few people have reported traveling through time.

☐ 3. Scientists have invented a way to make time travel happen.

☐ 4. People who experience time slips do not remember the experience afterwards.

☐ 5. It is not known why, when, or how time slips occur.

☐ 6. Many people believe they have traveled through time.

3 EXPLORING NEW CITIES
LESSON A ▶ *Popular destinations*

1 GRAMMAR

Underline the relative clauses in the postcard. Then add commas where necessary.

July 15

Dear Mom and Dad,

Greetings from Maine where the water is too cold for us to go swimming, but the scenery is beautiful. We're having a great time, and we've enjoyed every place that we've visited. This week we're in Bar Harbor which is a lovely island town. The place is absolutely full of tourists! Tonight we're going for a ride on a boat that will take us to one of the nearby islands. Our friend James who lives here has already taken us hiking and to the Bar Harbor Music Festival. It's been fun! That's it for now. We miss you.

Love, Sara and Eric

2 GRAMMAR

Join the following sentences using non-defining relative clauses.

1. Many tourists enjoy seeing the Kuala Lumpur skyline in Malaysia. It includes some of the tallest skyscrapers in the world.

    Many tourists enjoy seeing the Kuala Lumpur skyline in Malaysia,
    which includes some of the tallest skyscrapers in the world.

2. People visit Washington, D.C., in the spring. They can see the cherry trees in bloom then.

    _____

    _____

3. The cherry trees in Washington, D.C., were a gift from the Japanese government to the U.S. They are admired by everyone.

    _____

    _____

4. Thousands of years ago, people in Mexico began to grow corn. Corn continues to be a very important food in Mexico today.

    _____

    _____

5. The tortilla is typically eaten in Mexico. It is a thin, flat bread.

    _____

VOCABULARY

Choose the correct words to complete the sentences.

1. When preparing to host the 2012 Olympics, London updated its *hotels / climate /* (*transportation system*) with improvements to its subway.

2. New York City has hundreds of restaurants offering a wide variety of *climates / cuisines / green spaces*, including Italian, Chinese, and Indian.

3. Many people are moving from bigger cities to smaller towns because the *cost of living / landmark / climate* is more affordable.

4. If you enjoy *neighborhoods / shopping / nightlife*, you'll love the music and live shows in Rio de Janeiro.

5. Some people think Reykjavik, Iceland, is cold in the wintertime, but surprisingly, it has a very mild *climate / cuisine / transportation system* during the winter months.

6. Some famous *green spaces / neighborhoods / landmarks* in Paris include the Eiffel Tower and the Louvre Museum.

7. Many cities are preserving *green spaces / hotels / cuisines* in their downtown areas for people to have picnics, walk their dogs, and enjoy outdoor concerts.

GRAMMAR

Use defining or non-defining relative clauses to write sentences about these topics.

- a popular tourist activity in your city
- a town with many historical attractions
- a place with a good climate
- an excellent city for shopping

1. *Tourists in Rome like to visit the famous squares, which have many beautiful statues and fountains.*

2. _____
   _____
   _____
   _____

3. _____
   _____

4. _____
   _____

WRITING

A Look at the words and phrases in the box about Chiang Mai, Thailand.
Choose the main idea and write it in the center of the mind map. Then
write the supporting details in the mind map.

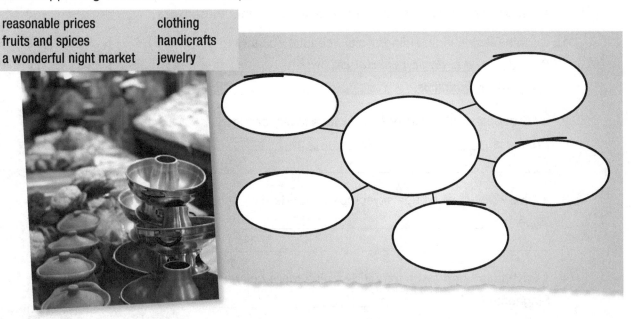

reasonable prices   clothing
fruits and spices   handicrafts
a wonderful night market jewelry

B Now read the paragraph about Chiang Mai. Answer the questions.

Chiang Mai is a city in northern Thailand that has a wonderful night market. In the evening, the main street is lined with small stands and shops that sell almost anything you can imagine. Some stands sell jewelry or clothing, others sell traditional Thai handicrafts, and still others sell fresh fruit and spices. I love spicy Thai food. It's easy to spend an entire evening just looking at everything. If you decide to buy something, you won't be disappointed. The prices are very reasonable. There are a lot of wonderful attractions in Chiang Mai, but the night market is a favorite for many people.

1. What is this paragraph about? _____

2. What is the topic sentence of the paragraph? _____
_____

3. Which sentence does not support the main idea? Cross it out.

C Write a paragraph about one of the places you mentioned in Exercise 4 on page 14.
Include a topic sentence with the main idea and several supporting ideas.

_____
_____
_____
_____
_____

1 GRAMMAR

Unscramble the words to complete the sentences about these cities.

1. a / with fascinating buildings / city / coastal / charming
Salvador is _a charming coastal city with_
fascinating buildings.

2. a / European / city / quaint / old / with a lovely castle
Prague is _____

_____

3. a / lively / city / with huge skyscrapers / modern
Taipei is _____

_____

4. a / dynamic / port / with trendy shopping malls / city
Singapore is _____

_____

5. a / industrial / modern / large / city / with a beautiful lakeshore
Chicago is _____

6. an / with world-famous theme parks / tourist / exciting / destination
Orlando is _____

2 VOCABULARY

Choose the word that best completes each sentence.

| border | coastal | college | mountain | port | rural | tourist |

1. Ana lives in a _____rural_____ town. The nearest big city is more than two hours away.

2. The local university employs most of the people living in this _____ town.

3. _____ towns are near an ocean, a lake, or a river where ships unload cargo.

4. People traveling from the U.S. to Mexico through _____ towns must stop and show their passports or other identification.

5. I work in a small _____ town with great beaches and seafood places.

6. We stopped in a crowded _____ town full of overpriced souvenir shops.

7. Nick lives in a _____ town that is nearly 3,000 meters above sea level.

3 GRAMMAR

Rewrite the sentences using the words in parentheses.

1. The streets are well lit, but it's best to be careful at night. (in spite of)
   In spite of the well-lit streets, it's best to be careful at night.

2. There is a crime problem, but it's still a wonderful place to visit. (despite)
   _____

3. The shopping malls are crowded, but people aren't buying much. (although)
   _____

4. It snows a lot, but I still like living here. (even though)
   _____

5. My city is on the ocean, but the water here is too polluted for people to go swimming. (however)
   _____

6. The city center is very picturesque, but there's not much to do. (nevertheless)
   _____

7. There's a lot to do here at night, but it's a very noisy neighborhood. (on the other hand)
   _____

4 GRAMMAR

Complete the sentences with your own opinions about cities you know.

1. The worst thing about ____*Los Angeles*____ is ____*the heavy traffic*____.
   In spite of that, *it is an ideal place to live* _____.

2. The worst thing about _____ is _____.
   Nevertheless, _____.

3. The best thing about _____ is _____.
   However, _____.

4. Even though _____ has a lot of _____,
   _____.

5. The weather in _____ is _____.
   On the other hand, _____.

6. _____ would be a great place to live. However, _____
   _____.

7. Although _____ is a favorite tourist destination for many, it also has its
   problems. For example, _____.

5 READING

A Match the words in the box with the photos. Then read two articles about megacities.

> auto emissions   carpooling   a landfill   public transportation

1. _carpooling_   2. _____   3. _____   4. _____

MEGACITIES: TWO VIEWS

1 The world's population is not only growing, it is also becoming more urbanized. An increasing number of people are moving to cities in the hope of having a better life. The cities promise steady work and higher salaries. With more money, people think they can provide for their families more easily.

As the population becomes more urbanized, megacities are created. Yes, there are more jobs in urban areas, but is the quality of life better in these megacities? A quick survey of several major cities reveals some of their problems: Pollution from auto emissions is poisoning the air; landfills are overflowing with garbage. With declining resources and growing competition, sometimes there is not enough food. These are all very serious problems.

We cannot get rid of megacities – they are here to stay. What we should concentrate on, however, is building "villages" inside the cities. These "urban villages" could be self-sufficient and grow their own food. The members of these villages would recycle more and do less damage to the environment. The villages would serve the needs of the local people, not big business. We need to limit large-scale development, not encourage it.

2 It's true that megacities have problems, but these have been exaggerated. The truth of the matter is that people move to cities to escape their hard life in the country. Urban areas, even with their problems, offer people a better life than rural areas. The old ways of life in rural areas have broken down, and it is now very difficult to make a living as a farmer.

People live longer in the cities. Medical care is better. And, of course, employment opportunities can be found more easily in the city. We should continue to develop city services so that people can enjoy their lives in the world's urban centers.

Rather than limiting development, we should encourage it. Public transportation systems need to be developed so that people can travel to and from work and school easily. Carpooling should be encouraged to cut down on pollution. The more we clean up and develop our megacities, the more life will improve for the residents.

> **megacity**
> a city with a population of 10 million or more

B Match the statements with the articles that support them.

	1	2	1 & 2
1. "Megacities have problems."	☐	☐	☐
2. "Life in rural areas is hard."	☐	☐	☐
3. "We should recreate village life in the cities."	☐	☐	☐
4. "There are more chances to work in the cities."	☐	☐	☐
5. "Continued development will hurt the quality of life."	☐	☐	☐
6. "Continued development can improve the quality of life."	☐	☐	☐

1 GRAMMAR

Combine the sentences using the words in parentheses. Use reduced time clauses wherever possible.

1. Classes are over for the day. I often go out with my friends. (after)
   After classes are over for the day, I often go out with my friends.

2. I lost my watch. I've been late for all my appointments. (ever since)
   _____

3. You should relax and count to 10. You start to feel stressed. (as soon as)
   _____

4. I go for a run. I stretch for at least 15 minutes. (right before)
   _____

5. She shouldn't listen to music. She is studying for a big test. (while)
   _____

6. I watch TV. I fall asleep. (until)
   _____

7. I get to the office. I start planning what I need to do that day. (from the moment)
   _____

2 GRAMMAR

Read the statements. Are they true for you? Choose true or false. Then rewrite the false statements to make them true.

	True	False
1. Whenever I get stressed out, I take a walk and try to relax.	☐	☑

   I usually eat a lot of snacks whenever I get stressed out.

| 2. As soon as I wake up, I check my email and phone messages. | ☐ | ☐ |

   _____

| 3. Ever since I started studying English, I've spoken more confidently. | ☐ | ☐ |

   _____

| 4. I like to read the news while I'm eating lunch. | ☐ | ☐ |

   _____

| 5. After I fall asleep, nothing can wake me up. | ☐ | ☐ |

   _____

VOCABULARY

Use the phrasal verbs from the box to complete the conversations.

| |
| burn out |
| calm down |
| chill out |
| doze off |
| perk up |
| turn in |

1. A: I lost my car keys! I'm going to be late for my doctor's appointment!
   B: You need to ___*calm down*___. Relax. Maybe you can reschedule.

2. A: You look tired. You need to _____ before our meeting.
   B: Yeah, you're right. Maybe I should have a cup of coffee.

3. A: Poor Jenny. She has two papers to write and a final exam to study for.
   B: That's a lot of work. I hope she doesn't _____ before graduation.

4. A: My flight leaves tomorrow morning at six o'clock.
   B: You should _____ early tonight so you'll wake up on time.

5. A: What a day! I had three meetings and a business lunch. I'm so tired.
   B: Let's have some dinner. Then let's _____ and watch TV.

6. A: Oh, sorry! I guess I fell asleep.
   B: You should go to bed earlier. Then you wouldn't _____ in class.

GRAMMAR

Use time clauses to complete the sentences so they are true for you.

1. __*As soon as*___ I get home from work, I __*change into some comfortable clothes*___
   _*and make dinner.*___

2. _____ I have the chance to chill out, I _____

   _____

3. _____ I met my best friend, we _____

   _____

4. _____ I started riding a bike, I _____

   _____

5. _____ eating a large meal, I _____

   _____

5 WRITING

A Read the paragraph and choose the best topic sentence. Is each topic sentence too general, too specific, or just right? Choose the correct answer.

1. _____

We experience a gradual rise of energy in the morning, peaking around noon. There is a slow decline in energy in the midafternoon with a second peak early in the evening. This is followed by a steady decline in energy until bedtime. Everyone experiences these energy patterns. They are a part of daily life.

	Too general	Too specific	Just right
a. People need energy to get through the day.	☐	☐	☐
b. People's energy patterns change according to the time of day.	☐	☐	☐
c. Everyone's energy peaks around noon.	☐	☐	☐

2. _____

Newborn babies sleep an average of 15 to 18 hours a day, but as children grow older, they sleep less. However, as teenagers, they seem to need a lot of sleep again. It is not unusual for teens to sleep until noon on weekends if their parents let them. As people age beyond their thirties, they tend to sleep less and less and for shorter periods of time.

	Too general	Too specific	Just right
a. People's sleep needs change as they go through life.	☐	☐	☐
b. Babies sleep more than elderly people.	☐	☐	☐
c. Everyone needs sleep.	☐	☐	☐

3. _____

In fact, Americans now spend close to $30 billion a year on vitamins and food supplements. Vitamin companies supply an almost endless variety of vitamins. There are multivitamins for adults, special vitamins for women, flavored vitamins for children, and even vitamins to help students study better. New types of vitamins come out regularly, and at least one store in every shopping mall sells vitamins.

	Too general	Too specific	Just right
a. Vitamins supplement a healthy diet.	☐	☐	☐
b. Vitamins are popular with women.	☐	☐	☐
c. In the U.S., vitamins are big business.	☐	☐	☐

B Write a topic sentence about how to keep your energy up or sleep well. Then write a paragraph that supports your main idea.

_____

_____

1 VOCABULARY

Rewrite the sentences by replacing the underlined words with phrases from the box.
Sometimes more than one answer is possible.

be fast asleep
be sound asleep
be wide awake
drift off
feel drowsy
have a sleepless night
nod off
sleep like a log
take a power nap
toss and turn

1. If Elisa is worried when she goes to bed, she is <u>unable to sleep</u>.

   If Elisa is worried when she goes to bed, she tosses and turns.

   If Elisa is worried when she goes to bed, she has a sleepless night.

2. My father always <u>falls asleep</u> after eating a heavy meal.

   _____

3. Simon often <u>sleeps for a few minutes</u> to boost his creativity at work.

   _____

4. The loud music didn't wake Sue. She must <u>be in a deep sleep</u>.

   _____

5. Liz is lucky she <u>sleeps heavily</u> because her roommate snores so loudly!

   _____

6. Marina isn't tired at all. In fact, she <u>is completely alert</u>!

   _____

7. Kenji often <u>begins to feel sleepy</u> when he reads on the train or in a car.

   _____

2 GRAMMAR

Choose the word or phrase that best completes each sentence.

1. *Considering that / Just in case /* (*Unless*) I'm really worried, I usually sleep well.
2. *Even if / Just in case / Only if* I have bad dreams, I don't recall the details later.
3. *Even if / As long as / Unless* I sleep well, I wake up feeling rested.
4. *Considering that / Only if / Unless* I didn't sleep last night, I feel pretty good.
5. Bring an umbrella with you *only if / as long as / just in case* it rains later.

3 GRAMMAR

Use the information in the box and the expressions in parentheses to write new sentences.

> I drink too much caffeine during the day.
> I forget to set my alarm clock.
> I get thirsty in the middle of the night.
> I sleep deeply.
> I'm completely exhausted.
> I've slept well the night before.

1. I always feel great in the morning. (as long as)

   I always feel great in the morning as long as I've slept well the night before.

2. Sometimes I have trouble drifting off. (even if)

   _____

3. My neighbors listen to loud music every night. (considering that)

   _____

4. I never oversleep in the morning. (unless)

   _____

5. I keep a glass of water by my bed. (just in case)

   _____

6. I have trouble falling asleep. (only . . . if)

   _____

4 GRAMMAR

Answer these questions using clauses with *as long as, considering that, even if, (just) in case, only . . . if,* or *unless.*

1. Do you stay awake thinking, or do you fall asleep as soon as you lie down?

   I only stay awake thinking if I'm having a problem at work.

2. Are you usually alert or still sleepy when you first get up in the morning?

   _____

3. Do you ever take naps during the day, or do you wait until bedtime to sleep?

   _____

4. Do you sleep like a log all night, or do you toss and turn?

   _____

5. Do you always need eight hours of sleep a night, or can you survive on less?

   _____

A Read the article quickly. Which three sleep theories are mentioned?

Why Sleep?

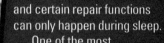

For some people, sleep is a great pleasure that they look forward to after a long day. For others, sleep is just a necessity, almost a waste of time. Regardless of where you stand, there's no denying that, at some point, everyone needs sleep. Without it, you'll find yourself irritable, confused, and lacking in energy. And the fact is that humans can survive longer without food than they can without sleep. But why is sleep necessary?

There are several theories that try to explain why sleep is so important. One of them, the energy conservation theory, suggests that a period of inactivity gives the body a chance to save energy. Basically, most mammals sleep through the night because instinct tells them it is less practical and more dangerous to hunt for or gather food in the dark. Another possible explanation is the restorative theory. According to this theory, the body needs time to repair itself after the physical efforts of the day, and certain repair functions can only happen during sleep.

One of the most fascinating discoveries about sleep is that it is not a period of total inactivity, as scientists previously believed. While we sleep, things are happening in the brain that researchers are only beginning to understand. The brain plasticity theory states that sleep is necessary to allow the brain to adjust to new experiences and information, and that a reorganization of the information in the brain takes place during sleep. Experts say that plenty of sleep the first night after learning a new skill or a new set of facts is crucial for improving memory and performance.

Dr. Robert Stickgold, a cognitive neuroscientist, says, "There's an old joke that the function of sleep is to cure sleepiness." Since there is no real agreement on a single reason for sleep, that may be the best explanation we have. Not to mention the fact that, after an exhausting day, it just feels good.

B Are the statements true or false? Choose the correct answer. Then rewrite the false statements to make them true.

	True	False
1. Humans need food more than they need sleep.	☐	☐
_____		
2. The conservation and restorative theories are concerned more with physical than mental processes.	☐	☐
_____		
3. Scientists have always believed there is brain activity during sleep.	☐	☐
_____		
4. Scientists have a complete understanding of what happens in the brain during sleep.	☐	☐
_____		
5. According to the brain plasticity theory, sleeping well after learning something new will help you remember it.	☐	☐
_____		

5 COMMUNICATION

LESSON A ► *Making conversation*

1 GRAMMAR

Are these customs similar to or different from customs in your culture? Choose your answer.
For the customs that are different, write an explanation.

	Similar	Different
1. It's customary in India to take your shoes off when entering a home.	☐	☐

In my culture, _____

_____

2. In Greece, it's not unusual to kiss friends and relatives on both cheeks when meeting them.	☐	☐

_____

_____

3. In some countries, owning a pet like a dog, a cat, or a bird is considered inappropriate.	☐	☐

_____

_____

4. In the U.S., arriving 30 minutes early to a dinner party isn't a good idea.	☐	☐

_____

_____

2 VOCABULARY

Choose the word or phrase that best describes how each situation is viewed in your culture.
Then write a sentence about the custom.

1. saying hello to strangers (appropriate / inappropriate /(normal))
   Saying hello to strangers in my culture is considered normal. _____

2. opening a door for someone (bad form / polite / strange)
   _____

3. splitting a restaurant bill with a friend (a compliment / an insult / typical)
   _____

4. offering your seat on a bus to a child (normal / offensive / unusual)
   _____

5. chewing with your mouth open (polite / rude / typical)
   _____

③ GRAMMAR

Use the information in the chart to make sentences about the dos and don'ts of customs in the U.S. Use the infinitive form of the verb in your answers.

Customs in the U.S.	
Dos	**Don'ts**
Acceptable: Use hand gestures while speaking.	Inappropriate: Talk about religion or politics.
Not unusual: Ask people how they feel.	Not a good idea: Ask about someone's salary.
Customary: Ask what someone does for a living.	Rude: Tell someone he or she has gained weight.

1. *It's acceptable to use hand gestures while speaking.* _____

2. _____

3. _____

4. _____

5. _____

6. _____

④ GRAMMAR

Use gerunds to rewrite the sentences you wrote above.

1. *Using hand gestures while speaking is acceptable.* _____

2. _____

3. _____

4. _____

5. _____

6. _____

⑤ GRAMMAR

What should people know about your customs? Write sentences with infinitive phrases or gerunds.

1. meeting business associates

When you meet business associates in my culture,
it's typical to exchange business cards.
When you meet business associates in my culture,
exchanging business cards is typical.

2. getting married

_____

_____

_____

_____

3. eating out _____

_____

6 WRITING

A Read the parts of a paragraph about small talk. They have been mixed up. Put them in the correct order according to the outline.

1. _____ Topic sentence
2. _____ Supporting sentences: General example
3. _____ Supporting sentences: Personal example
4. _____ Concluding sentence

a For example, personal income is seen as too private to be a suitable topic for small talk in the U.S. People in the U.S. normally avoid asking other people how much they make, and they rarely offer information about their own salary.

b Small talk is common in every culture, but the topics that are considered suitable or unsuitable vary from country to country.

c In conclusion, when dealing with people from other cultures, it's a good idea to be aware of which topics are considered suitable and avoid those that aren't – in that way, you can avoid creating the kind of awkwardness that small talk is meant to reduce.

d I remember being very taken aback when, at a party, a person from another country asked me what I did for a living and then asked me how much money I made. My inability to answer right away made me realize that this really is a taboo topic in our culture, if not in others. After some hesitation, and hoping I didn't sound rude, my answer was, "Oh, enough to support myself."

B Think of a topic of small talk that is avoided in your country or a country you know well. Write notes for a short paragraph about the topic using the outline below.

1. Topic sentence: _____

2. Supporting sentences:

    2.1 General example: _____

    2.2 Personal example: _____

3. Concluding sentence: _____

C Write a paragraph about the topic using the outline and your notes above.

_____
_____
_____
_____
_____
_____
_____

GRAMMAR

Read Victoria and Alicia's conversation about a movie star. Then read the sentences below. One mistake is underlined in each sentence. Rewrite the sentences with the correct verb tenses.

Victoria: Did you see the new *Star Monthly*? Jenny Roberts bought an amazing new house!

Alicia: When did she buy it?

Victoria: She moved in last week.

Alicia: Lucky Jenny. Is she happy?

Victoria: Actually, she's not. That's what it says here in *Star Monthly*.

Alicia: Really? Let me see that.

Victoria: Yeah. She found out the closets are too small!

1. Victoria told Alicia that Jenny Roberts <u>did buy</u> a new house.
   Victoria told Alicia that Jenny Roberts had bought a new house.

2. Alicia asked Victoria when she <u>was buying</u> it.
   _____

3. Victoria told Alicia that she <u>was moving in</u> last week.
   _____

4. Alicia asked Victoria if Jenny <u>is</u> happy.
   _____

5. Victoria told Alicia that Jenny <u>will not be</u> happy.
   _____

6. Victoria told Alicia that Jenny <u>has found out</u> the closets were too small.
   _____

2 GRAMMAR

Read the conversation. Use reported speech to complete the sentences.

Mark: Sandra, sit down. Did you hear about Paul Alvaro?

Sandra: No, I didn't. What happened?

Mark: He got a promotion.

Sandra: When did it happen?

Mark: Yesterday. The official announcement will be made soon.

1. Mark told Sandra _to sit down._ _____
2. He asked her _____
3. She said that _____
4. She asked Mark _____
5. Mark said that Paul _____
6. Sandra asked Mark _____
7. Mark said that it _____
8. He said that the official announcement _____

3 VOCABULARY

Use the expressions in the box to complete the blog entry. Sometimes more than one answer is possible.

she claimed that	she explained that	she warned me not to
she encouraged me to	she told us that	she wondered

November 10

My technology teacher gave us a difficult assignment today. (1) _____ *She told us that* _____
we had to prepare a 10-minute oral presentation for Friday. I can't stand speaking in front of the
class. Anyway, I asked my teacher if I could do a different assignment – like a written report.
(2) _____ why I didn't want to do the presentation, so I told her
how nervous I get when I have to speak in class.

(3) _____ she couldn't change the assignment for me. But she did
have some advice. (4) _____ put off the assignment. Then
(5) _____ practice my presentation with a friend.
(6) _____ if I practiced my presentation ahead of time, I would feel
more comfortable on the day I actually had to give it. So, I hope Rita can come over tomorrow
and listen to my presentation. Are you reading this, Rita? Please say "yes"!

COMMENTS (12)   SHARE THIS

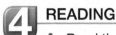

A Read the article. Find the boldfaced words that match the definitions.

1. problems _____*pitfalls*_____
2. increase _____
3. unclear _____
4. concern for others _____
5. talking too proudly about yourself _____
6. not thinking you are better than others _____

How nice of you to say so . . .

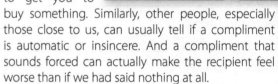

Everyone appreciates a compliment. They are expressions of admiration, acceptance, and affection that make the recipient of the compliment feel good and **boost** positive feelings in the giver of the compliment as well. Friendships and good working relationships alike can develop out of a well-worded and appropriately timed compliment. As in most areas of social interaction, though, giving and receiving compliments can present problems. What's meant to be positive can turn out to be offensive unless you're aware of the possible **pitfalls**.

One point that many of us forget – or perhaps never realized – is that the best compliments are specific. Instead of a quick "Good job!" to a colleague or classmate, mentioning how well organized their presentation was, or how it taught you something new, will have the greatest effect. Similarly, try to avoid **vague** language like, "Wow, you got a new haircut!" If the recipient of your intended compliment is feeling unsure about this new look, they might think: ". . . and it looks terrible!" Explain what's good about it or why it's an improvement so there is no misunderstanding.

Sincerity is also important when it comes to compliments. When salespeople tell you how great you look or how smart you seem, you can often tell if they really mean it or if they are just trying to get you to buy something. Similarly, other people, especially those close to us, can usually tell if a compliment is automatic or insincere. And a compliment that sounds forced can actually make the recipient feel worse than if we had said nothing at all.

How you receive a compliment can also determine if the exchange will be a positive or a negative one. Many people reject compliments by saying, "Oh, it was nothing," or "It wasn't me – Tom did all the work." This may seem like the right, and **humble**, thing to do. Accepting a compliment with no argument can feel like **boasting** to many people and in many cultures. However, in the U.S. and most Western cultures, graciously accepting a positive statement with a simple thank-you shows the other person that you respect their judgment and appreciate their **thoughtfulness**. So the next time someone comments on your new outfit, try to resist saying you bought it for next to nothing, it doesn't fit well and, anyway, your sister picked it out. Just smile, say thank you, and accept it as a positive moment for both of you.

B Read the article again. Choose the correct answers.

1. The author believes that giving compliments . . .
   - ☐ a. always has a positive effect.
   - ☐ b. can present problems.
   - ☐ c. isn't complicated.

2. According to the article, an unclear compliment . . .
   - ☐ a. is as good as a specific one.
   - ☐ b. always causes offense.
   - ☐ c. can be misunderstood.

3. According to the article, some salespeople might use compliments in order to . . .
   - ☐ a. make themselves feel better.
   - ☐ b. influence your decision.
   - ☐ c. appear humble.

4. In the U.S., rejecting a compliment gives the impression that . . .
   - ☐ a. you don't respect the giver.
   - ☐ b. you are boasting.
   - ☐ c. you feel insecure.

6 WHAT'S THE REAL STORY?

LESSON A ▶ *That's some story!*

1 GRAMMAR

Choose the sentences with grammatical mistakes. Rewrite them using the correct verb forms.

☑ 1. A government spokesperson has announced new economic policies yesterday.
   A government spokesperson announced new economic policies yesterday.

☐ 2. Unusual weather events have been happening across the country.
   _____

☐ 3. Police arrested several identity thieves so far this year.
   _____

☐ 4. Burglars have stolen two paintings on Monday night.
   _____

☐ 5. Several observers saw a rare butterfly in Central Park over the past week.
   _____

☐ 6. Jazz pianist Jacqueline Gray gave a concert at the Civic Center last night.
   _____

☐ 7. The stock market has fallen sharply the other day.
   _____

2 GRAMMAR

Choose the verbs that best complete this update about an ongoing news story.

UPDATED 8:12 A.M.

The County Municipal Airport (1) *has delayed* / *has been delaying* a flight to London. The delay (2) *has occurred* / *has been occurring* because airline personnel (3) *have been trying* / *tried* to locate a snake inside the plane. While information is incomplete at this time, we do know a few things. As flight attendants were preparing for takeoff, several passengers saw a snake under their seats. The pilot alerted the flight control tower, and the flight was delayed in order to find the snake. Crew members (4) *have searched* / *have been searching* the plane ever since. They still (5) *haven't been locating* / *haven't located* the snake, and no one (6) *has come up* / *has been coming up* with an explanation as to how it got there. Technicians (7) *have removed* / *have been removing* a section of the cabin floor to see if it may have hidden there. All the passengers (8) *have left* / *have been leaving* the plane already. They (9) *have sat* / *have been sitting* inside the terminal enjoying free soft drinks and snacks.

3 VOCABULARY

Match these headlines with the news events in the box.

epidemic	kidnapping	political crisis	recession	scandal
hijacking	natural disaster	rebellion	robbery	

Millions Found in Director's Secret Bank Account

1. _____scandal_____

$1.5 Million Stolen!

2. _____

Airline Passengers Still Being Held Captive

3. _____

Earthquake Destroys Houses Downtown

4. _____

Prime Minister Resigns!

5. _____

Virus Sickens Thousands

6. _____

Hundreds of Inmates Take Over Prison

7. _____

Millionaire's Wife Held for Ransom

8. _____

Stocks and Employment Numbers Fall

9. _____

4 GRAMMAR

Complete these sentences about some of the headlines above with your own ideas. Use the present perfect or present perfect continuous form of the verbs in parentheses.

1. Officials say the director (withdraw) *has been withdrawing hundreds of thousands of dollars from the company account for the past three years.*

   The director (deny) *has denied stealing any money.*

2. A bank robber (steal) _____

   _____

   The bank robber (hide) _____

3. Passengers on Flight 200 (hold) _____

   _____

   The hijackers (demand) _____

4. The earthquake (destroy) _____

   _____

   Many people (volunteer) _____

5 WRITING

A Read the news story. Then number the pictures in the correct order.

a.

b.

c.

d.

Trapped Cat Rescued

After spending 14 days trapped inside the walls of a 157-year-old building in New York City last April, Molly briefly became a world-famous cat. Attempting to save the black cat, rescuers set traps and used special cameras and a raw fish to try to lure Molly out from between the walls. They even tried using kittens to appeal to the cat's motherly side so she would come out, but Molly would not budge.

Finally, after they removed bricks and drilled holes into the walls, someone was able to pull the curious cat out of the tiny space.

The bricks have now been replaced, but Molly has been getting visits from tourists daily since she was rescued. Even so, Molly's adventures may not be over. Her owners say that at least once they have caught her looking inside a similar hole in the building.

B Read the story again. Underline the present perfect and present perfect continuous verbs.

C Write a news story about an interesting recent event. Use the present perfect, present perfect continuous, and simple past.

_____

_____

_____

_____

_____

_____

_____

GRAMMAR

Choose the correct expressions to complete the sentences.

1. She was amazed when she won the competition. *The moment /
   The next day /* Until that time, she had never won anything.

2. I felt awful about breaking my friend's phone. *Afterwards / When /
   Until that time*, I offered to replace it.

3. Despite my fear, I loved flying. *The moment / Up until then / Later*,
   I had never been on an airplane.

4. On Saturday, my mother left an urgent message on my voice mail.
   Until that time / Later / As soon as I got it, I called her back.

5. I had a delicious meal at a restaurant on Sunday. *The next day / When /
   Up until then*, however, I woke up with a serious case of food poisoning.

6. When I walked into the room, everyone yelled "Happy birthday!" *As soon as /
   Before that / Afterwards*, I'd never had a surprise party.

7. I got a big promotion at work. *Until that time / When / Later*, while I was telling
   my family, I felt really proud.

 GRAMMAR

Complete the sentences. Use the past perfect or the simple past of the verbs in parentheses.

1. I couldn't figure out why she looked so familiar. Later, I ____*realized*____ (realize) she
   was my sixth-grade teacher.

2. I knew it was the delivery person knocking on my door. As soon as I _____
   (open) the door, he _____ (give) me a big package.

3. While hiking, we suddenly realized we were lost and didn't have a compass or GPS.
   Up until then, we _____ (not be) worried.

4. I had never experienced anything so exciting. Until that time, my life _____ (be)
   very uneventful.

5. I went to the airport and booked the next flight. Afterwards, I _____ (wait) for
   the announcement to board the plane.

6. It was my first time running a marathon. When I _____ (see) the finish line in
   front of me, I _____ (feel) relieved.

7. I finally passed my driving test. The moment I _____ (receive) my driver's
   license in the mail, I _____ (begin) to dance.

8. My father was moved by the performance. Before that, I _____ (never see)
   him cry.

3 VOCABULARY

Use the expressions from the boxes to complete the conversation.

| it all started when | the next thing we knew | the thing you have to know is |

Mia: Hi, Ben. I heard you and Luke got lost on your way to the big game.

Ben: Yeah. (1) ___*It all started when*___ we began singing along with this cool song.

Mia: What happened?

Ben: Well, we were having such a good time that, (2) _____, we'd missed the turn for the stadium.

Mia: How did you do that?

Ben: (3) _____, when I'm singing a song I really like, I don't pay attention to anything around me.

| I forgot to mention that | meanwhile | the other thing was |

Mia: So you were having such a good time you didn't notice you'd gone past your turn?

Ben: That's about right. (4) _____, we'd driven about 40 miles too far!

Mia: Forty miles? Wow!

Ben: And (5) _____, we ran out of gas.

Mia: You ran out of gas? On the highway?

Ben: No, not on the highway. (6) _____ we'd decided to take a shortcut.

| I forgot to mention that | to make a long story short |

Mia: Did you make it to the game?

Ben: Yes. But it took us about three hours to get there!

Mia: Are you kidding?

Ben: (7) _____ we also stopped for pizza.

Mia: Seriously?

Ben: Well, getting lost made us hungry! So, (8) _____, we only saw the last half hour of the game.

4 READING

A Read the anecdotes about strange weather events. Then write brief summaries.

Susan's strange weather event was _____

_____

Elena's strange weather event was _____

_____

WACKY *Weather Stories*

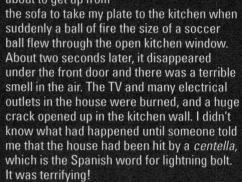

Last summer, I was working at home on a sunny day. For some reason, I had gone around to the front of the house to get something. As I did, I felt some drops on my face, which soon developed into a very heavy shower. A few seconds later, I went to the back of the house and realized that it was totally dry there. The shower was only at the front of the house and not at the back. I stood in the hallway and looked one way – pouring – and the other way – sunny and dry. After a few minutes, the downpour stopped entirely. Up until then, I'd never seen such strange weather.

— **Susan, United States**

One spring day, I was sitting in the living room of my farmhouse in Uruguay watching TV and having lunch. I had just finished eating and was about to get up from the sofa to take my plate to the kitchen when suddenly a ball of fire the size of a soccer ball flew through the open kitchen window. About two seconds later, it disappeared under the front door and there was a terrible smell in the air. The TV and many electrical outlets in the house were burned, and a huge crack opened up in the kitchen wall. I didn't know what had happened until someone told me that the house had been hit by a *centella,* which is the Spanish word for lightning bolt. It was terrifying!

— **Elena, Uruguay**

B Choose true or false. Then rewrite the false statements to make them true.

	True	False
1. It was already pouring when Susan went to the front of the house.	☐	☐
2. Susan witnessed two kinds of weather at the same time.	☐	☐
3. The rain soon spread to both sides of Susan's house.	☐	☐
4. The fireball caused actual damage to Elena's house.	☐	☐
5. Elena understood immediately what had happened.	☐	☐